Every Problem Is Alw[...]
Wisdom Problem.

When Your Heart Decides The
Destination, Your Mind Will
Design The Map To Reach It.

2

What You Respect,
You Will Attract.

3

The Secret Of Your Future Is
Hidden In Your Daily Routine.

4

Your Rewards In Life Are
Determined By The Kinds
Of Problems You Are Willing
To Solve For Others.

5

What You Make Happen For
Others, God Will
Make Happen For You.

6

An Uncommon Seed Always
Creates An Uncommon
Harvest.

7

8 The Word Of God Is
The Wisdom Of God.

9 The Clearer Your Goals,
The Greater Your Faith.

10 Your Focus Decides
Your Feelings.

11 Your Self-Portrait Determines
Your Self-Conduct.

12 Your Respect For Time
Is A Prediction Of Your
Financial Future.

13 Your Decisions Decide
Your Wealth.

14 The Instruction You Follow
Determines The Future
You Create.

God's Only Pain Is To Be Doubted; God's Only Pleasure Is To Be Believed.

15

Your Goals Choose Your Mentors.

16

Your Success Is Decided By What You Are Willing To Ignore.

17

The Atmosphere You Create Determines The Product You Produce.

18

The Size Of Your Enemy Determines The Size Of Your Rewards.

19

Your Assignment Is Always The Problem God Has Designed You To Solve For Others.

20

What You Are Willing To Walk Away From Determines What God Will Bring To You.

21

22 **Y**our Future Is Decided By Who You Choose To Believe.

23 **C**hanges In Your Life Will Always Be Proportionate To Your Knowledge.

24 **T**he Reward Of Pain Is The Willingness To Change.

25 **A**nything Permitted Increases.

26 **A**nything That Keeps Your Attention Has Become Your Master.

27 **Y**our Life Is Whatever You Choose To Remember.

28 **W**hen You Want Something You Have Never Had, You Must Do Something You Have Never Done.

What You Repeatedly Hear,
You Eventually Believe.

29

All Men Fall, The Great
Ones Get Back Up.

30

You Cannot Correct
What You Are Unwilling
To Confront.

31

You Will Only Be
Remembered In Life For Two
Things: The Problems You Solve
Or The Ones You Create.

32

God Never Consults
Your Past To Decide
Your Future.

33

Any Movement Towards
Order Creates Pleasure.

34

If You Insist On Taking
Something God Did Not Give
You, He Will Take Back
Something He Gave You.

35

5

36 The Evidence Of God's Presence Far Outweighs The Proof Of His Absence.

37 Never Complain About What You Permit.

38 Go Where You Are Celebrated Instead Of Where You Are Tolerated.

39 One Day Of Favor Is Worth A Thousand Days Of Labor.

40 Warfare Always Surrounds The Birth Of A Miracle.

41 The Broken Become Masters At Mending.

42 Prosperity Is Simply Having Enough Of God's Provision To Complete His Assignment In Your Life.

One Hour In The Presence Of God Will Reveal The Flaws Of Your Most Carefully Laid Plans.

43

Anger Is The Birthplace For Solutions.

44

The Willingness To Reach Births The Ability To Change.

45

Never Give More Time To A Critic Than You Would Give To A Friend.

46

Access Is First A Gift, Then A Test, Then A Reward.

47

The Magnetism Of Your Kindness Will Outlast The Memory Of Your Genius.

48

When You Let Go Of What Is In Your Hand, God Let's Go Of What Is In His Hand.

49

7

50 Never Rewrite Your Theology To Accommodate A Tragedy.

51 Crisis Always Occurs At The Curve Of Change.

52 You Never Outgrow Warfare; You Must Simply Learn To Fight.

53 Memory Is More Enslaving Than Any Injustice.

54 Your Significance Is Not In Your Similarity To Another, But In Your Point Of Difference From Another.

55 What You Can Tolerate, You Cannot Change.

56 The Seasons Of Your Life Will Change Every Time You Use Your Faith.

When You Ask God For A Miracle, He Will Always Give You An Instruction.

57

Whatever Is Missing In Your Life Is Something You Have Not Truly Valued.

58

Your Reaction To Greatness Reveals Your Humility.

59

Honor Is The Seed For Longevity, Of Life Or Friendship.

60

Your Words Are The Seeds For Feelings.

61

Friends Create Comfort; Enemies Create Change.

62

Something In Your Hand Can Create Anything You Want In Your Future.

63

64 Your Unwillingness To Trust The Right Person Will Create More Losses Than Your Mistake Of Trusting The Wrong Person.

65 Anything Good Is Hated By Everything Evil.

66 An Uncommon Dream Will Require An Uncommon Mentor.

67 What Saddens You Is A Clue To What God Has Assigned You To Heal.

68 Every Environment Requires A Code Of Conduct For Entering Or Remaining In It.

69 Greatness Is Not The Absence Of A Flaw—But The Willingness To Overcome It.

70 Each Act Of Obedience Shortens The Distance To Any Miracle You Are Pursuing.

Your Reaction To The Word Of God Is A Picture Of Your Respect For God.

71

The Problem That Infuriates You The Most Is The Problem God Has Assigned You To Solve.

72

False Accusation Is The Last Stage Before Supernatural Promotion.

73

Miracles Happen As Quickly As Tragedies.

74

The Difference Between Significance And Insignificance Is An Adversary.

75

When Wrong People Leave Your Life, Wrong Things Stop Happening.

76

Seed-Faith Is Sowing Something You Have Been Given For Something Else You Have Been Promised.

77

78 Disobedience Is Always More Costly Than Obedience.

79 An Uncommon Enemy Will Require Uncommon Wisdom.

80 What You Say Is Not As Important As What Others Remember.

81 Never Discuss Your Problem With Someone Incapable Of Solving It.

82 Joy Is The Divine Reward For Discerning The Divine Purpose Of The Immediate Moment.

83 God Never Responds To Pain, But He Always Responds To Pursuit.

84 When You Get Involved With God's Dream, He Will Get Involved With Your Dream.

The True Function
Of Wisdom Is Order.

85

Confrontation Is
The Attempt To Preserve
A Relationship.

86

The Wise Never Discuss
What They Want Others
To Forget.

87

The Proof Of Love Is The
Passion To Pleasure.

88

Pain Is The Proof
Of Disorder.

89

Debt Is The Proof
Of Greed.

90

Giving Is The Only Proof You
Have Conquered Greed.

91

92 If Time Heals,
God Is Unnecessary.

93 Loneliness Is Not The
Absence Of Affection, But
The Absence Of Direction.

94 Money Is Merely A Reward
For Solving Problems.

95 Access Becomes A
Continuous Test.

96 When Fatigue Walks In,
Faith Walks Out.

97 Patience Is The Weapon
That Forces Deception
To Reveal Itself.

98 Any Step Toward
Self-Sufficiency Is
A Step Away From God.

Ignorance Is The Only Weapon Satan Can Effectively Use Against You.

99

A Tired Mind Rarely Makes Good Decisions.

100

An Uncommon Dream Requires Uncommon Patience.

101

Anything You Do Not Have Is Stored In Someone Near You, And Love Is The Secret Map To The Treasure.

102

The Proof Of Mediocrity Is The Resentment Of Excellence.

103

Conduct Permitted Is Conduct Taught.

104

A Seed Of Nothing Always Creates A Season Of Nothing.

105

106 Mentorship Is Wisdom Without The Pain.

107 An Unconquered Weakness Always Births A Tragedy.

108 Anger Is Simply Passion Requiring An Appropriate Focus.

109 Bitterness Is Deadlier Than Betrayal.

110 An Uncommon Assignment Attracts An Uncommon Adversary.

111 Gifts Reveal The Character Of Those Who Receive Them.

112 Giving Is Emptying Your Present To Fill Up Your Future.

Obedience Is The Only Thing God Has Ever Required Of Man.

113

Business Is Simply Solving A Problem For An Agreed Reward.

114

Currents Of Favor Begin To Flow The Moment You Solve A Problem For Someone.

115

Champions Are Willing To Walk Away From Something They Desire To Protect Something Else They Love.

116

An Uncontested Enemy Will Flourish.

117

God Creates Seasons; Discoveries Schedule Them.

118

God Had A Son But He Wanted A Family; He Sowed His Son To Create His Family.

119

120 God Sent His Son,
But He Left His Book.

121 Champions Are Willing To Do
Things They Hate To Create
Something Else They Love.

122 Everything God Created Is
A Solution To A Problem.

123 Every Friendship Nurtures
A Strength Or A Weakness.

124 Bad Times Bring
Good People Together.

125 One Day Of Doubt Will
Create 365 Days Of Pain.

126 God Will Never Ask For
Something You Don't Have; He
Will Always Ask For Something
You Want To Keep.

Order Is God's
Only Obsession.

127

Creativity Is The Search For
Options; Focus Is The
Elimination Of Them.

128

If You Don't Know Where You
Belong, You Will Adapt To
Where You Are.

129

Give Another What He
Cannot Find Anywhere Else
And He Will Keep Returning.

130

Endurance Demoralizes
Your Adversary.

131

Miracles Do Not Go Where
They Are Needed; They Go
Where They Are Expected.

132

If What You Hold In Your
Hand Is Not Enough To Be
Your Harvest, It Must Be Your
Seed.

133

134 Access Creates Demands; Demands Create Expectations; Expectations Create Distraction; Distraction Creates Failure.

135 Debt Is Emptying Your Future To Fill Up Your Present.

136 Provision Is Only Guaranteed At The Place Of Your Assignment.

137 God Disguises His Greatest Gifts In The Most Flawed Vessels So Only The Most Passionate Qualify To Receive Them.

138 Losers Focus On What They Are Going Through; Champions Focus On What They Are Going To.

139 Silence Cannot Be Misquoted.

140 Money Does Not Change You; It Magnifies What You Already Are.

The Holy Spirit Is The Only Person Capable Of Being Completely Satisfied With You.

141

Diligence Is Immediate Attention To An Assigned Task.

142

Restlessness Is Your Future Whimpering At Your Feet Begging For Instructions.

143

God Will Never Authorize A Man To Marry A Woman Who Refuses To Follow; Nor A Woman To Marry A Man Who Refuses To Lead.

144

Men Do Not Drown By Falling In The Water; They Drown By Staying There.

145

The Purpose Of Memory Is To Revisit Places Of Pleasure.

146

Nothing Leaves Heaven Until Something Leaves Earth.

147

21

148 The Holy Spirit Is The Only Person You Are Required To Obey.

149 Failure Is Not An Event, But Merely An Opinion.

150 Stop Looking At Where You Have Been And Start Looking At Where You Can Be.

151 What You Say Determines What God Is Willing To Do For You.

152 Pain Is Not Your Enemy— Merely The Proof That You Have One.

153 Flattery Is Speaking Good Words For Wrong Reasons.

154 Only A Fool Negotiates With A Giver.

The Person Of Jesus Creates Your Peace; The Principles Of Jesus Create Your Prosperity.

155

Fame Will Birth Pursuit; Pursuit Will Birth Demands; Demands Will Birth Distractions; Distractions Will Birth Failure.

156

The Only Reason Men Fail Is Broken Focus.

157

Jealousy Is Believing Another Received What You Deserved.

158

The Waves Of Yesterday's Disobedience Will Splash On The Shores Of Tomorrow For A Season.

159

The Quality Of A Nation Is Revealed By The Quality Of The Leader God Permits To Govern Them.

160

Something You Already Have Can Create Anything Else You Will Ever Want.

161

162 The Presence Of God Is The Only Place Where Your Weakness Will Die.

163 Focus Creates Blindness.

164 The Pain Of Your Past Will Decide Your Passion For The Future.

165 Nobody Is Ever As They First Appear.

166 Satan Always Attacks Those Next In Line For A Promotion.

167 The Quickest Cure For Ingratitude Is Loss.

168 The Anointing You Respect Is The Anointing That Increases In Your Life.

The Price God Was Willing To Pay Reveals The Worth Of The Product He Saw.

169

Anything Unrecognized Becomes Unrewarded; Anything Unrewarded... Will Exit.

170

The Problem Closest To You Is Your Door Out Of Trouble.

171

Parasites View Your Weakness As A Reason To Leave; Protégés View Your Weakness As A Reason To Stay.

172

Satan's Favorite Entry Point Into Your Life Is Always Through Someone Close To You.

173

The Ungodly Give Gifts To Influence Decisions; The Godly Give Gifts To Prove Love.

174

The Difference Between Seasons Is Simply An Instruction.

175

176 The Price Of God's Presence Is Time.

177 Information Births Confidence.

178 The Problem You Are Willing To Solve Determines Who Pursues You.

179 Parasites Want What You Have *Earned*—Protégés Want What You Have *Learned*.

180 Struggle Is The Proof That You Have Not Yet Been Conquered.

181 Those Without Your Memories Cannot Feel Your Pain.

182 Your Seed Will Expose The Character Of The Soil.

The Three Rewards For Christ
Are Forgiveness, A Friend
And A Future.

183

Integrity Cannot Be Proven,
Only Discerned.

184

The Problems You Solve
Determine The Rewards
You Receive.

185

People Don't Always
Remember What You Say,
They Always Remember How
They Felt When You Said It.

186

The Goal Of An Enemy
Is To Change
Your Self-Portrait.

187

Time Will Expose What
Interrogation Cannot.

188

The Quality Of The Soil
Determines The Future
Of The Seed.

189

190 The Will Of God Is An Attitude, Not A Place.

191 Make Your Future So Big Yesterday Disappears.

192 The Quality Of Your Questions Will Determine The Quality Of Your Discoveries.

193 Popularity Is When People Like You; Happiness Is When You Like You.

194 True Friends Have The Same Enemies.

195 To Love Something Is To Find It Desirable; To Respect Something Is To Find It Valuable.

196 The Quality Of Your Seed Determines The Quality Of Your Harvest.

197 The Workings Of God Are Never Proportionate To Your Need Of Him, But Proportionate To Your Knowledge Of Him.

198 May You Never Have Anything God Is Unwilling To Give.

199 The Season For Research Is Not The Season For Marketing.

200 Someone In Trouble Is Always Your Door Out Of Trouble.

201 Warfare Is The Proof Your Enemy Has Discerned Your Future.

202 What You Hear Determines What You Become Willing To Change.

203 The Seed That Leaves Your Hand Never Leaves Your Life; It Enters Your Future Where It Multiplies.

204 There Are Two Ways To Increase Wisdom: Mistakes And Mentors.

205 Tired Eyes Rarely See A Good Future.

206 Those Comfortable With Your Weakness May Be Adversarial Toward Your Assignment.

207 Someone Is Always Observing You Who Is Capable Of Greatly Blessing You.

208 What You Cannot Hate— You Cannot Conquer.

209 Whatever You Are Attempting To Live Without Is Something You Do Not Yet Truly Value.

210 Tithe Is Not The Payment Of A Debt—But The Acknowledgement Of It.

Uncommon Obedience
Unleashes Uncommon Favor.

211

Never Complain About Your
Present If You Are Unwilling
To Walk Toward Your Future.

212

Those Who Ask
The Questions Determine
The Quality
Of The Conversation.

213

Submission Cannot Begin
Until Agreement Ends.

214

When Satan Wants
To Destroy You, He Puts
A Person In Your Life.

215

When You Can Manage
A Day, You Can Manage
Your Life.

216

Tithe Is The Proof Of Your
Obedience; Offering Is Proof
Of Your Generosity.

217

218 What Enters You Determines What Exits You.

219 Nothing Is Ever As Bad As It First Appears.

220 Those Who Impart Knowledge Are Also Capable Of Imparting Error.

221 That Which Becomes Familiar Becomes Hidden.

222 When You Ask God For A Promotion, He Will Schedule An Adversary.

223 When You Replay The Past, You Poison The Present.

224 What You Do First Determines What God Does Second.

What Happens In
Your Mind Usually
Happens In Time.

225

Nothing Will Ever Dominate
Your Life Unless It Happens
Daily.

226

Those Who Unlock Your
Compassion Are Those
To Whom You Have
Been Assigned.

227

The Kindest Word Is
An Unkind Word Unsaid.

228

When You Delay A Battle,
You Delay Your Rewards.

229

Yesterday Is In The Tomb,
Tomorrow Is In The Womb—
The Only Place You Will Ever
Be Is Today.

230

What You Do Is
What You Believe.

231

232 What You Do Daily Determines What You Become Permanently.

233 Package Yourself For Where You Are Going Instead Of Where You Have Been.

234 What Grieves You Is A Clue To Something You Were Assigned To Heal.

235 The Longevity Of Every Relationship Is Decided By The Willingness To Forgive.

236 When You Discover Your Assignment, You Will Discover Your Enemy.

237 You Have No Right To Anything You Have Not Pursued.

238 Whatever You Have Been Given Is Enough To Create Anything Else You Have Been Promised.

What You Hear Determines
What You Feel.

239

People See What You
Are Before They Hear
What You Are.

240

What You Hate Reveals What
You Were Created To Correct.

241

The Proof Of Humility
Is The Willingness To Reach.

242

Wrong People Birth
Sad Seasons.

243

Your Chosen Focus Is
The World You Have Created
For Yourself.

244

Whatever You Sow Is Your
Seed; Whatever You Keep Is
Your Harvest.

245

246 The Battle Of Life Is For Your Mind; The Battle Of The Mind Is For Focus.

247 Protocol Will Take You Further Than Genius.

248 What You Love The Most Is A Clue To The Gift You Contain.

249 The Proof Of Love Is The Desire To Give.

250 Your Assignment Will Always Have An Adversary.

251 What You Hear Determines What You Pursue.

252 When God Talks To You About A Seed, He Has A Harvest On His Mind.

When You Ignore God, You Schedule A Tragedy. **253**

Successful Men Do Daily What Unsuccessful Men Do Occasionally. **254**

You Are Never Responsible For The Pain Of Those Who Have Ignored Your Counsel. **255**

The Proof Of Love Is The Obsession To Protect. **256**

Your Goals Force Every Adversary To Express Their Opposition To You. **257**

Fathers Decide What Daughters Remember; Mothers Decide What Sons Believe. **258**

When You Ask God For A Harvest, He Will Always Ask You For A Seed. **259**

260 Mentorship Creates Success Without The Waiting.

261 The Atmosphere You Create Determines The Future Of Your Weakness.

262 You Will Only Remember Something You Teach.

263 The Proof Of Love Is The Willingness To Change.

264 Your Self-Portrait Determines The Kind Of Enemy You Are Willing To Confront.

265 Where You Are Determines What Dies Within You.

266 When You Open Your Hands, God Will Open His Windows.

Where You Are Determines What Grows Within You— Your Weakness Or Your Strength.

267

The First Step Toward Success Is The Willingness To Listen.

268

You Cannot Be What You Are Not, But You Can Become What You Are Not.

269

The Proof Of Love Is The Willingness To Correct.

270

The Importance Of Your Assignment Is Revealed By The Intensity Of Your Adversity.

271

The Proof Of Love Is The Willingness To Listen.

272

When You Sow What You Have Been Given, You Will Reap What You Have Been Promised.

273

39

274 Where You Are Determines What You Hear; What You Hear Determines What You Believe.

275 The Greatest Success Quality On Earth Is The Willingness To Become.

276 Your Reactions Reveal Your Character.

277 The Proof Of Loyalty Is The Unwillingness To Betray.

278 Your Enemies Decide Your Promotions.

279 Your Attitude Determines Your Access.

280 You Can Create With Your Seed What You Cannot Buy With Your Money.

The Attitude Of The Servant Decides The Atmosphere Of The Palace.

281

The Most Dangerous Person In Your Life Is The One Who Feeds Your Doubts.

282

You Will Never Be Promoted Until You Become Over-Qualified For Your Present Assignment.

283

The Proof Of Order Is The Absence Of Strife.

284

Crisis Is Simply An Invitation To A Miracle.

285

Never Gaze At Something That Does Not Belong In Your Future.

286

Your Seed Is A Photograph Of Your Faith.

287

288 Where You Are Determines Who Sees You.

289 The Proof Of Desire Is Pursuit.

290 You Will Only Have Significant Success With Something That Is An Obsession.

291 The Proofs Of Legitimate Authority Are Provision, Protection And Promotion.

292 Honor Must Become Your Seed Before You Reap It As A Harvest.

293 Distrust Destroys Passion.

294 Your Seed Is Anything That Benefits Another; Your Harvest Is Anything That Benefits You.

Worship Is The Correction
Of Focus.

2 9 5

The Pursuit Of The Mentor
Reveals The Passion
Of The Protégé.

2 9 6

Your Assignment Is Not Your
Decision—But Your Discovery.

2 9 7

Exposure Of Incompetence
Usually Births An Adversary.

2 9 8

The Right Thing At The
Wrong Time Becomes
The Wrong Thing.

2 9 9

Where You Are
Matters As Much
As What You Are.

3 0 0

Your Seed Is The Only
Influence You Have
Over Your Future.

3 0 1

302
Your Understanding Of God Determines Your Message To Men.

303
The Proof Of Prosperity Is The Ability To Lend; The Proof Of Impatience Is The Willingness To Borrow.

304
The Reward Of Submission Is Equal To The Reward Of Agreement.

305
God Gives You A Family To Prepare You For An Enemy.

306
What You Are Will Outlast What Men Say You Are.

307
The Proof Of Respect Is The Investment Of Time.

308
Your Tithe Is The Proof Of Your Trust.

You Cannot Have A Great Life Unless You Have A Pure Life; You Cannot Have A Pure Life Unless You Have A Pure Mind; You Cannot Have A Pure Mind Unless You Wash It Daily With The Word Of God.

309

Your Belief System Was Chosen For Comfort Or Change.

310

The Secret To Knowing A Man Is To Know His Memories.

311

Loss Is The First Step Toward Change.

312

Winners Are Simply Ex-Losers Who Got Mad.

313

The Reward Of Pain Is The Willingness To Listen.

314

The Anointing You Sow Into Is The Anointing You Reap From.

315

316 Parasites Want What Is In Your Hand; Protégés Want What Is In Your Heart.

317 Every Miracle Begins With A Conversation.

318 The Unthankful Are Always The Unhappy.

319 The Only Thing You Will Ever Need To Know Is What To Do Next.

320 Your Future Is Decided By What You Are Willing To Change.

321 Those Pursuing Greatness Are Worthy Of Pursuit.

322 You Will Only Be Remembered For Your Obsession.

The Person Of Jesus Prepares You For Eternity; The Principles Of Jesus Prepare You For Earth.

323

When You Get Involved With God's Family, He Will Get Involved With Your Family.

324

Those Who Cannot Increase You Will Inevitably Decrease You.

325

Loss Is The First Step Toward Discovering God.

326

Your Goals Allow Your Friends To Confirm Their Loyalty.

327

Those Who Habitually Disagree With Your Decisions Eventually Become Capable Of Disloyalty.

328

Your Faith Decides Your Miracles.

329

330 Greatness Is Simply Fulfilling God's Expectations Of You.

331 Those Who Disagree With Your Goals Will Usually Disagree With Your Decisions.

332 Those Who Sin With You Will Eventually Sin Against You.

333 You Are Never As Far From A Miracle As It First Appears.

334 Your Self-Portrait Determines What You Are Willing To Endure.

335 Intolerance Of Your Present Schedules Your Future.

336 Ecstasy To A Giver Is Discovering Someone Qualified To Receive.

Order Is Simply The Accurate Arrangement Of Things.

337

An Uncommon Future Requires An Uncommon Mentor.

338

What You Love Will Eventually Reward You.

339

You Can Only Conquer Something You Hate.

340

The Proof Of Impatience Is Debt.

341

Champions Make Decisions That Create *The Future* They Desire; Losers Make Decisions That Create *The Present* They Desire.

342

Anything You Do In An Attempt To Please God Will Not Go Unrewarded.

343

344 Your Reaction To A Man Of God Determines God's Reaction To You.

345 God Will Never Advance Your Instructions Beyond Your Last Act Of Disobedience.

346 Those Who Lie For You Will Eventually Lie Against You.

347 When God Wants To Bless You, He Brings A Person Into Your Life.

348 Your Pain Decides Your Goals.

349 Your Memory Replays Your Past; Your Imagination Preplays Your Future.

350 If You Must Believe Somebody, Believe Somebody Good.

An Uncommon Future Will Require Uncommon Preparation.

351

Your Reaction To An Instruction Determines The Access You Receive.

352

Those Who Do Not Respect Your Time Will Not Respect Your Wisdom Either.

353

When God Wants To Protect You, He Removes A Person From Your Life.

354

Your Unwillingness To Submit Deprives God Of The Authorization To Protect.

355

Those Without Your Pain Rarely Understand Your Goals.

356

An Uncommon Dream Requires Uncommon Faith.

357

358 What You Celebrate—
You Will Remember.

359 The Most Valuable Person In
Your Life Is The One Who
Feeds Your Faith.

360 Those Who Disrespect Your
Assignment Are Unqualified
For Access.

361 When You Agree With
A Rebel, You Reap
His Consequences.

362 Your Experiences Decide
Your Persuasions.

363 Your Reaction To Someone
In Trouble Determines God's
Reaction To You.

364 What You Can Walk Away
From You Have Mastered;
What You Cannot Walk Away
From Has Mastered You.

Anything Broken Can Be Repaired; Anything Closed Can Be Opened; Anything Lost Can Be Recovered.

365 Wisdom Keys of Mike Murdock
ISBN 1-56394-301-8/B-229
Copyright © 1994 by **MIKE MURDOCK**
All publishing rights belong exclusively to Wisdom International
Publisher/Editor: Deborah Murdock Johnson
Published by The Wisdom Center
4051 Denton Hwy. · Ft. Worth, TX 76117
1-817-759-BOOK · 1-817-759-0300

You Will Love Our Website...! WisdomOnline.com

Accuracy Department: To our Friends and Partners...We welcome any comments on errors or misprints you find in our book...Email our department: AccuracyDept@thewisdomcenter.tv. Your aid in helping us excel is highly valued.

ALPHABETIZED
WISDOM KEYS

1. A Seed Of Nothing Always Creates A Season Of Nothing. (#105)

2. A Tired Mind Rarely Makes Good Decisions. (#100)

3. Access Becomes A Continuous Test. (#95)

4. Access Creates Demands; Demands Create Expectations; Expectations Create Distraction; Distraction Creates Failure. (#134)

5. Access Is First A Gift, Then A Test, Then A Reward. (#47)

6. All Men Fall, The Great Ones Get Back Up. (#30)

7. An Uncommon Assignment Attracts An Uncommon Adversary. (#110)

8. An Uncommon Dream Requires Uncommon Patience. (#101)

9. An Uncommon Dream Will Require An Uncommon Mentor. (#66)

10. An Uncommon Dream Requires Uncommon Faith. (#357)

11. An Uncommon Enemy Will Require Uncommon Wisdom. (#79)

12. An Uncommon Future Requires An Uncommon Mentor. (#338)

13. An Uncommon Future Will Require Uncommon Preparation. (#351)

14. An Uncommon Seed Always Creates An Uncommon Harvest. (#7)

15. An Uncontested Enemy Will Flourish. (#117)

16. An Unconquered Weakness Always Births A Tragedy. (#107)

17. Anger Is Simply Passion Requiring An Appropriate Focus. (#108)

18. Anger Is The Birthplace For Solutions. (#44)

19. Any Movement Towards Order Creates Pleasure. (#34)

20. Any Step Toward Self-Sufficiency Is A Step Away From God. (#98)

21. Anything Broken Can Be Repaired; Anything Closed Can Be Opened; Anything Lost Can Be Recovered. (#365)

22. Anything Good Is Hated By Everything Evil. (#65)

23. Anything Permitted Increases. (#25)

24. Anything That Keeps Your Attention Has Become Your Master. (#26)

25. Anything Unrecognized Becomes Unrewarded, Anything Unrewarded...Will Exit. (#170)

26. Anything You Do In An Attempt To Please God Will Not Go Unrewarded. (#343)

27. Anything You Do Not Have Is Stored In Someone Near You, And Love Is The Secret Map To The Treasure. (#102)

28. Bad Times Bring Good People Together. (#124)

29. Bitterness Is Deadlier Than Betrayal. (#109)

30. Business Is Simply Solving A Problem For An Agreed Reward. (#114)

31. Champions Are Willing To Do Things They Hate To Create Something Else They Love. (#121)

32. Champions Are Willing To Walk Away From Something They Desire To Protect Something Else They Love. (#116)

33. Champions Make Decisions That Create The Future They Desire; Losers Make Decisions That Create The Present They Desire. (#342)

34. Changes In Your Life Will Always Be Proportionate To Your Knowledge. (#23)

35. Conduct Permitted Is Conduct Taught. (#104)

36. Confrontation Is The Attempt To Preserve A Relationship. (#86)

37. Creativity Is The Search For Options; Focus Is The Elimination Of Them. (#128)

38. Crisis Always Occurs At The Curve Of Change. (#51)

39. Crisis Is Simply An Invitation To A Miracle. (#285)

40. Currents Of Favor Begin To Flow The Moment You Solve A Problem For Someone. (#115)

41. Debt Is Emptying Your Future To Fill Up Your Present. (#135)

42. Debt Is The Proof Of Greed. (#90)

43. Diligence Is Immediate Attention To An Assigned Task. (#142)

44. Disobedience Is Always More Costly Than Obedience. (#78)

45. Distrust Destroys Passion. (#293)

46. Each Act Of Obedience Shortens The Distance To Any Miracle You Are Pursuing. (#70)

47. Ecstasy To A Giver Is Discovering Someone Qualified To Receive. (#336)

48. Endurance Demoralizes Your Adversary. (#131)

49. Every Environment Requires A Code Of Conduct For Entering Or Remaining In It. (#68)

50. Every Friendship Nurtures A Strength Or A Weakness. (#123)

51. Every Miracle Begins With A Conversation. (#317)

52. Every Problem Is Always A Wisdom Problem. (#1)

53. Everything God Created Is A Solution To A Problem. (#122)

54. Exposure Of Incompetence Usually Births An Adversary. (#298)

55. Failure Is Not An Event, But Merely An Opinion. (#149)

56. False Accusation Is The Last Stage Before Supernatural Promotion. (#73)

57. Fame Will Birth Pursuit; Pursuit Will Birth Demands; Demands Will Birth Distractions; Distractions Will Birth Failure. (#156)

58. Fathers Decide What Daughters Remember; Mothers Decide What Sons Believe. (#258)

59. Flattery Is Speaking Good Words For Wrong Reasons. (#153)

60. Focus Creates Blindness. (#163)

61. Friends Create Comfort; Enemies Create Change. (#62)

62. Gifts Reveal The Character Of Those Who Receive Them. (#111)
63. Give Another What He Cannot Find Anywhere Else And He Will Keep Returning. (#130)
64. Giving Is Emptying Your Present To Fill Up Your Future. (#112)
65. Giving Is The Only Proof You Have Conquered Greed. (#91)
66. Go Where You Are Celebrated Instead Of Where You Are Tolerated. (#38)
67. God Creates Seasons; Discoveries Schedule Them. (#118)
68. God Disguises His Greatest Gifts In The Most Flawed Vessels So Only The Most Passionate Qualify To Receive Them. (#137)
69. God Gives You A Family To Prepare You For An Enemy. (#305)
70. God Had A Son But He Wanted A Family; He Sowed His Son To Create His Family. (#119)
71. God Never Consults Your Past To Decide Your Future. (#33)
72. God Never Responds To Pain, But He Always Responds To Pursuit. (#83)
73. God's Only Pain Is To Be Doubted; God's Only Pleasure Is To Be Believed. (#15)
74. God Sent His Son, But He Left His Book. (#120)
75. God Will Never Advance Your Instructions Beyond Your Last Act Of Disobedience. (#345)
76. God Will Never Ask For Something You Don't Have; He Will Always Ask For Something You Want To Keep. (#126)
77. God Will Never Authorize A Man To Marry A Woman Who Refuses To Follow; Nor A Woman To Marry A Man Who Refuses To Lead. (#144)
78. Greatness Is Not The Absence Of A Flaw—But The Willingness To Overcome It. (#69)
79. Greatness Is Simply Fulfilling God's Expectations Of You. (#330)

80. Honor Is The Seed For Longevity, Of Life Or Relationships. (#60)
81. Honor Must Become Your Seed Before You Reap It As A Harvest. (#292)
82. If Time Heals, God Is Unnecessary. (#92)
83. If What You Hold In Your Hand Is Not Enough To Be Your Harvest, It Must Be Your Seed. (#133)
84. If You Don't Know Where You Belong, You Will Adapt To Where You Are. (#129)
85. If You Insist On Taking Something God Did Not Give You, He Will Take Back Something He Gave You. (#35)
86. If You Must Believe Somebody, Believe Somebody Good. (#350)
87. Ignorance Is The Only Weapon Satan Can Effectively Use Against You. (#99)
88. Information Births Confidence. (#177)
89. Integrity Cannot Be Proven, Only Discerned. (#184)
90. Intolerance Of Your Present Schedules Your Future. (#335)
91. Jealousy Is Believing Another Received What You Deserved. (#158)
92. Joy Is The Divine Reward For Discerning The Divine Purpose Of The Immediate Moment. (#82)
93. Loneliness Is Not The Absence Of Affection, But The Absence Of Direction. (#93)
94. Losers Focus On What They Are Going Through; Champions Focus On What They Are Going To. (#138)
95. Loss Is The First Step Toward Change. (#312)
96. Loss Is The First Step Toward Discovering God. (#326)
97. Make Your Future So Big Yesterday Disappears. (#191)
98. May You Never Have Anything God Is Unwilling To Give. (#198)
99. Memory Is More Enslaving Than Any Injustice. (#53)
100. Men Do Not Drown By Falling In The Water; They Drown By Staying There. (#145)

101. Mentorship Creates Success Without The Waiting. (#260)
102. Mentorship Is Wisdom Without The Pain. (#106)
103. Miracles Happen As Quickly As Tragedies. (#74)
104. Miracles Do Not Go Where They Are Needed; They Go Where They Are Expected. (#132)
105. Money Does Not Change You; It Magnifies What You Already Are. (#140)
106. Money Is Merely A Reward For Solving Problems. (#94)
107. Never Complain About What You Permit. (#37)
108. Never Complain About Your Present If You Are Unwilling To Walk Toward Your Future. (#212)
109. Never Discuss Your Problem With Someone Incapable Of Solving It. (#81)
110. Never Gaze At Something That Does Not Belong In Your Future. (#286)
111. Never Give More Time To A Critic Than You Would Give To A Friend. (#46)
112. Never Rewrite Your Theology To Accommodate A Tragedy. (#50)
113. Nobody Is Ever As They First Appear. (#165)
114. Nothing Is Ever As Bad As It First Appears. (#219)
115. Nothing Leaves Heaven Until Something Leaves Earth. (#147)
116. Nothing Will Ever Dominate Your Life Unless It Happens Daily. (#226)
117. Obedience Is The Only Thing God Has Ever Required Of Man. (#113)
118. One Day Of Doubt Will Create 365 Days Of Pain. (#125)
119. One Day Of Favor Is Worth A Thousand Days Of Labor. (#39)
120. One Hour In The Presence Of God Will Reveal The Flaws Of Your Most Carefully Laid Plans. (#43)
121. Only A Fool Negotiates With A Giver. (#154)
122. Order Is God's Only Obsession. (#127)

123. Order Is Simply The Accurate Arrangement Of Things. (#337)

124. Package Yourself For Where You Are Going Instead Of Where You Have Been. (#233)

125. Pain Is Not Your Enemy—Merely The Proof That You Have One. (#152)

126. Pain Is The Proof Of Disorder. (#89)

127. Parasites View Your Weakness As A Reason To Leave; Protégés View Your Weakness As A Reason To Stay. (#172)

128. Parasites Want What Is In Your Hand; Protégés Want What Is In Your Heart. (#316)

129. Parasites Want What You Have Earned—Protégés Want What You Have Learned. (#179)

130. Patience Is The Weapon That Forces Deception To Reveal Itself. (#97)

131. People Don't Always Remember What You Say, They Always Remember How They Felt When You Said It. (#186)

132. People See What You Are Before They Hear What You Are. (#240)

133. Popularity Is When People Like You; Happiness Is When You Like You. (#193)

134. Prosperity Is Simply Having Enough Of God's Provision To Complete His Assignment In Your Life. (#42)

135. Protocol Will Take You Further Than Genius. (#247)

136. Provision Is Only Guaranteed At The Place Of Your Assignment. (#136)

137. Restlessness Is Your Future Whimpering At Your Feet Begging For Instructions. (#143)

138. Satan Always Attacks Those Next In Line For A Promotion. (#166)

139. Satan's Favorite Entry Point Into Your Life Is Always Through Someone Close To You. (#173)

140. Seed-Faith Is Sowing Something You Have Been Given For Something Else You Have Been Promised. (#77)
141. Silence Cannot Be Misquoted. (#139)
142. Someone In Trouble Is Always Your Door Out Of Trouble. (#200)
143. Someone Is Always Observing You Who Is Capable Of Greatly Blessing You. (#207)
144. Something In Your Hand Can Create Anything You Want In Your Future. (#63)
145. Something You Already Have Can Create Anything Else You Will Ever Want. (#161)
146. Stop Looking At Where You Have Been, And Start Looking At Where You Can Be. (#150)
147. Struggle Is The Proof That You Have Not Yet Been Conquered. (#180)
148. Submission Cannot Begin Until Agreement Ends. (#214)
149. Successful Men Do Daily What Unsuccessful Men Do Occasionally. (#254)
150. That Which Becomes Familiar Becomes Hidden. (#221)
151. The Anointing You Respect Is The Anointing That Increases In Your Life. (#168)
152. The Anointing You Sow Into Is The Anointing You Reap From. (#315)
153. The Atmosphere You Create Determines The Product You Produce. (#18)
154. The Atmosphere You Create Determines The Future Of Your Weakness. (#261)
155. The Attitude Of The Servant Decides The Atmosphere Of The Palace. (#281)
156. The Battle Of Life Is For Your Mind; The Battle Of The Mind Is For Focus. (#246)
157. The Broken Become Masters At Mending. (#41)
158. The Clearer Your Goals, The Greater Your Faith. (#9)

159. The Difference Between Seasons Is Simply An Instruction. (#175)

160. The Difference Between Significance And Insignificance Is An Adversary. (#75)

161. The Evidence Of God's Presence Far Outweighs The Proof Of His Absence. (#36)

162. The First Step Toward Success Is The Willingness To Listen. (#268)

163. The Goal Of An Enemy Is To Change Your Self-Portrait. (#187)

164. The Greatest Success Quality On Earth Is The Willingness To Become. (#275)

165. The Holy Spirit Is The Only Person Capable Of Being Completely Satisfied With You. (#141)

166. The Holy Spirit Is The Only Person You Are Required To Obey. (#148)

167. The Importance Of Your Assignment Is Revealed By The Intensity Of Your Adversity. (#271)

168. The Instruction You Follow Determines The Future You Create. (#14)

169. The Kindest Word Is An Unkind Word Unsaid. (#228)

170. The Longevity Of Every Relationship Is Decided By The Willingness To Forgive. (#235)

171. The Magnetism Of Your Kindness Will Outlast The Memory Of Your Genius. (#48)

172. The Most Dangerous Person In Your Life Is The One Who Feeds Your Doubts. (#282)

173. The Most Valuable Person In Your Life Is The One Who Feeds Your Faith. (#359)

174. The Only Reason Men Fail Is Broken Focus. (#157)

175. The Only Thing You Will Ever Need To Know Is What To Do Next. (#319)

176. The Pain Of Your Past Will Decide Your Passion For The Future. (#164)

177. The Person Of Jesus Creates Your Peace; The Principles Of Jesus Create Your Prosperity. (#155)

178. The Person Of Jesus Prepares You For Eternity; The Principles Of Jesus Prepare You For Earth. (#323)

179. The Presence Of God Is The Only Place Where Your Weakness Will Die. (#162)

180. The Price God Was Willing To Pay Reveals The Worth Of The Product He Saw. (#169)

181. The Price Of God's Presence Is Time. (#176)

182. The Problem Closest To You Is Your Door Out Of Trouble. (#171)

183. The Problem That Infuriates You The Most Is The Problem God Has Assigned You To Solve. (#72)

184. The Problem You Are Willing To Solve Determines Who Pursues You. (#178)

185. The Problems You Solve Determine The Rewards You Receive. (#185)

186. The Proof Of Desire Is Pursuit. (#289)

187. The Proof Of Humility Is The Willingness To Reach. (#242)

188. The Proof Of Impatience Is Debt. (#341)

189. The Proof Of Love Is The Desire To Give. (#249)

190. The Proof Of Love Is The Obsession To Protect. (#256)

191. The Proof Of Love Is The Passion To Pleasure. (#88)

192. The Proof Of Love Is The Willingness To Change. (#263)

193. The Proof Of Love Is The Willingness To Correct. (#270)

194. The Proof Of Love Is The Willingness To Listen. (#272)

195. The Proof Of Loyalty Is The Unwillingness To Betray. (#277)

196. The Proof Of Mediocrity Is The Resentment Of Excellence. (#103)

197. The Proof Of Order Is The Absence Of Strife. (#284)

198. The Proof Of Prosperity Is The Ability To Lend; The Proof Of Impatience Is The Willingness To Borrow. (#303)

199. The Proof Of Respect Is The Investment Of Time. (#307)

200. The Proofs Of Legitimate Authority Are Provision, Protection And Promotion. (#291)

201. The Purpose Of Memory Is To Revisit Places Of Pleasure. (#146)

202. The Pursuit Of The Mentor Reveals The Passion Of The Protégé. (#296)

203. The Quality Of A Nation Is Revealed By The Quality Of The Leader God Permits To Govern Them. (#160)

204. The Quality Of The Soil Determines The Future Of The Seed. (#189)

205. The Quality Of Your Questions Will Determine The Quality Of Your Discoveries. (#192)

206. The Quality Of Your Seed Determines The Quality Of Your Harvest. (#196)

207. The Quickest Cure For Ingratitude Is Loss. (#167)

208. The Reward Of Pain Is The Willingness To Change. (#24)

209. The Reward Of Pain Is The Willingness To Listen. (#314)

210. The Reward Of Submission Is Equal To The Reward Of Agreement. (#304)

211. The Right Thing At The Wrong Time Becomes The Wrong Thing. (#299)

212. The Season For Research Is Not The Season For Marketing. (#199)

213. The Seasons Of Your Life Will Change Every Time You Use Your Faith. (#56)

214. The Secret Of Your Future Is Hidden In Your Daily Routine. (#4)

215. The Secret To Knowing A Man Is To Know His Memories. (#311)

216. The Seed That Leaves Your Hand Never Leaves Your Life; It Enters Your Future Where It Multiplies. (#203)

217. The Size Of Your Enemy Determines The Size Of Your Rewards. (#19)

218. The Three Rewards For Christ Are Forgiveness, A Friend And A Future. (#183)

219. The True Function Of Wisdom Is Order. (#85)

220. The Ungodly Give Gifts To Influence Decisions; The Godly Give Gifts To Prove Love. (#174)

221. The Unthankful Are Always The Unhappy. (#318)

222. The Waves Of Yesterday's Disobedience Will Splash On The Shores Of Tomorrow For A Season. (#159)

223. The Will Of God Is An Attitude, Not A Place. (#190)

224. The Willingness To Reach Births The Ability To Change. (#45)

225. The Wise Never Discuss What They Want Others To Forget. (#87)

226. The Word Of God Is The Wisdom Of God. (#8)

227. The Workings Of God Are Never Proportionate To Your Need Of Him, But Proportionate To Your Knowledge Of Him. (#197)

228. There Are Two Ways To Increase Wisdom: Mistakes And Mentors. (#204)

229. Those Comfortable With Your Weakness May Be Adversarial Toward Your Assignment. (#206)

230. Those Pursuing Greatness Are Worthy Of Pursuit. (#321)

231. Those Who Ask The Questions Determine The Quality Of The Conversation. (#213)

232. Those Who Cannot Increase You Will Inevitably Decrease You. (#325)

233. Those Who Disagree With Your Goals Will Usually Disagree With Your Decisions. (#331)

234. Those Who Disrespect Your Assignment Are Unqualified For Access. (#360)

235. Those Who Do Not Respect Your Time Will Not Respect Your Wisdom Either. (#353)

236. Those Who Habitually Disagree With Your Decisions Eventually Become Capable Of Disloyalty. (#328)

237. Those Who Impart Knowledge Are Also Capable Of Imparting Error. (#220)
238. Those Who Lie For You Will Eventually Lie Against You. (#346)
239. Those Who Sin With You Eventually Sin Against You. (#332)
240. Those Who Unlock Your Compassion Are Those To Whom You Have Been Assigned. (#227)
241. Those Without Your Memories Cannot Feel Your Pain. (#181)
242. Those Without Your Pain Rarely Understand Your Goals. (#356)
243. Time Will Expose What Interrogation Cannot. (#188)
244. Tired Eyes Rarely See A Good Future. (#205)
245. Tithe Is Not The Payment Of A Debt—But The Acknowledgement Of It. (#210)
246. Tithe Is The Proof Of Your Obedience; Offering Is Proof Of Your Generosity. (#217)
247. To Love Something Is To Find It Desirable; To Respect Something Is To Find It Valuable. (#195)
248. True Friends Have The Same Enemies. (#194)
249. Uncommon Obedience Unleashes Uncommon Favor. (#211)
250. Warfare Always Surrounds The Birth Of A Miracle. (#40)
251. Warfare Is The Proof Your Enemy Has Discerned Your Future. (#201)
252. What Enters You Determines What Exits You. (#218)
253. What Grieves You Is A Clue To Something You Were Assigned To Heal. (#234)
254. What Happens In Your Mind Usually Happens In Time. (#225)
255. What Saddens You Is A Clue To What God Has Assigned You To Heal. (#67)
256. What You Are Will Outlast What Men Say You Are. (#306)

257. What You Are Willing To Walk Away From Determines What God Will Bring To You. (#21)

258. What You Can Tolerate, You Cannot Change. (#55)

259. What You Can Walk Away From You Have Mastered; What You Cannot Walk Away From Has Mastered You. (#364)

260. What You Cannot Hate—You Cannot Conquer. (#208)

261. What You Celebrate—You Will Remember. (#358)

262. What You Do Daily Determines What You Become Permanently. (#232)

263. What You Do First Determines What God Does Second. (#224)

264. What You Do Is What You Believe. (#231)

265. What You Hate Reveals What You Were Created To Correct. (#241)

266. What You Hear Determines What You Become Willing To Change. (#202)

267. What You Hear Determines What You Feel. (#239)

268. What You Hear Determines What You Pursue. (#251)

269. What You Love The Most Is A Clue To The Gift You Contain. (#248)

270. What You Love Will Eventually Reward You. (#339)

271. What You Make Happen For Others, God Will Make Happen For You. (#6)

272. What You Repeatedly Hear, You Eventually Believe. (#29)

273. What You Respect, You Will Attract. (#3)

274. What You Say Determines What God Is Willing To Do For You. (#151)

275. What You Say Is Not As Important As What Others Remember. (#80)

276. Whatever Is Missing In Your Life Is Something You Have Not Truly Valued. (#58)

277. Whatever You Are Attempting To Live Without Is Something You Do Not Yet Truly Value. (#209)

278. Whatever You Have Been Given Is Enough To Create Anything Else You Have Been Promised. (#238)
279. Whatever You Sow Is Your Seed; Whatever You Keep Is Your Harvest. (#245)
280. When Fatigue Walks In, Faith Walks Out. (#96)
281. When God Talks To You About A Seed, He Has A Harvest On His Mind. (#252)
282. When God Wants To Bless You, He Brings A Person Into Your Life. (#347)
283. When God Wants To Protect You, He Removes A Person From Your Life. (#354)
284. When Satan Wants To Destroy You, He Puts A Person In Your Life. (#215)
285. When Wrong People Leave Your Life, Wrong Things Stop Happening. (#76)
286. When You Agree With A Rebel, You Reap His Consequences. (#361)
287. When You Ask God For A Harvest, He Will Always Ask You For A Seed. (#259)
288. When You Ask God For A Miracle, He Will Always Give You An Instruction. (#57)
289. When You Ask God For A Promotion, He Will Schedule An Adversary. (#222)
290. When You Can Manage A Day, You Can Manage Your Life. (#216)
291. When You Delay A Battle, You Delay Your Rewards. (#229)
292. When You Discover Your Assignment, You Will Discover Your Enemy. (#236)
293. When You Get Involved With God's Dream, He Will Get Involved With Your Dream. (#84)
294. When You Get Involved With God's Family, He Will Get Involved With Your Family. (#324)
295. When You Ignore God, You Schedule A Tragedy. (#253)

296. When You Let Go Of What Is In Your Hand, God Let's Go Of What Is In His Hand. (#49)

297. When You Open Your Hands, God Will Open His Windows. (#266)

298. When You Replay The Past, You Poison The Present. (#223)

299. When You Sow What You Have Been Given, You Will Reap What You Have Been Promised. (#273)

300. When You Want Something You Have Never Had, You Must Do Something You Have Never Done. (#28)

301. When Your Heart Decides The Destination, Your Mind Will Design The Map To Reach It. (#2)

302. Where You Are Determines What Grows Within You— Your Weakness Or Your Strength. (#267)

303. Where You Are Determines What Dies Within You. (#265)

304. Where You Are Determines What You Hear; What You Hear Determines What You Believe. (#274)

305. Where You Are Determines Who Sees You. (#288)

306. Where You Are Matters As Much As What You Are. (#300)

307. Winners Are Simply Ex-Losers Who Got Mad. (#313)

308. Worship Is The Correction Of Focus. (#295)

309. Wrong People Birth Sad Seasons. (#243)

310. Yesterday Is In The Tomb, Tomorrow Is In The Womb— The Only Place You Will Ever Be Is Today. (#230)

311. You Are Never As Far From A Miracle As It First Appears. (#333)

312. You Are Never Responsible For The Pain Of Those Who Have Ignored Your Counsel. (#255)

313. You Can Create With Your Seed What You Cannot Buy With Your Money. (#280)

314. You Can Only Conquer Something You Hate. (#340)

315. You Cannot Be What You Are Not, But You Can Become What You Are Not. (#269)

316. You Cannot Correct What You Are Unwilling To Confront. (#31)

317. You Cannot Have A Great Life Unless You Have A Pure Life; You Cannot Have A Pure Life Unless You Have A Pure Mind; You Cannot Have A Pure Mind Unless You Wash It Daily With The Word Of God. (#309)

318. You Have No Right To Anything You Have Not Pursued. (#237)

319. You Never Outgrow Warfare; You Must Simply Learn To Fight. (#52)

320. You Will Never Be Promoted Until You Become Over-Qualified For Your Present Assignment. (#283)

321. You Will Only Be Remembered In Life For Two Things: The Problems You Solve Or The Ones You Create. (#32)

322. You Will Only Be Remembered For Your Obsession. (#322)

323. You Will Only Have Significant Success With Something That Is An Obsession. (#290)

324. You Will Only Remember Something You Teach. (#262)

325. Your Assignment Is Always The Problem God Has Designed You To Solve For Others. (#20)

326. Your Assignment Is Not Your Decision—But Your Discovery. (#297)

327. Your Assignment Will Always Have An Adversary. (#250)

328. Your Attitude Determines Your Access. (#279)

329. Your Belief System Was Chosen For Comfort Or Change. (#310)

330. Your Chosen Focus Is The World You Have Created For Yourself. (#244)

331. Your Decisions Decide Your Wealth. (#13)

332. Your Enemies Decide Your Promotions. (#278)

333. Your Experiences Decide Your Persuasions. (#362)

334. Your Faith Decides Your Miracles. (#329)

335. Your Focus Decides Your Feelings. (#10)

336. Your Future Is Decided By What You Are Willing To Change. (#320)

337. Your Future Is Decided By Who You Choose To Believe. (#22)

338. Your Goals Allow Your Friends To Confirm Their Loyalty. (#327)

339. Your Goals Choose Your Mentors. (#16)

340. Your Goals Force Every Adversary To Express Their Opposition To You. (#257)

341. Your Life Is Whatever You Choose To Remember. (#27)

342. Your Memory Replays Your Past; Your Imagination Preplays Your Future. (#349)

343. Your Pain Decides Your Goals. (#348)

344. Your Reaction To A Man Of God Determines God's Reaction To You. (#344)

345. Your Reaction To An Instruction Determines The Access You Receive. (#352)

346. Your Reaction To Greatness Reveals Your Humility. (#59)

347. Your Reaction To Someone In Trouble Determines God's Reaction To You. (#363)

348. Your Reaction To The Word Of God Is A Picture Of Your Respect For God. (#71)

349. Your Reactions Reveal Your Character. (#276)

350. Your Respect For Time Is A Prediction Of Your Financial Future. (#12)

351. Your Rewards In Life Are Determined By The Kinds Of Problems You Are Willing To Solve For Others. (#5)

352. Your Seed Is A Photograph Of Your Faith. (#287)

353. Your Seed Is Anything That Benefits Another; Your Harvest Is Anything That Benefits You. (#294)

354. Your Seed Is The Only Influence You Have Over Your Future. (#301)

355. Your Seed Will Expose The Character Of The Soil. (#182)

356. Your Self-Portrait Determines The Kind Of Enemy You Are Willing To Confront. (#264)

357. Your Self-Portrait Determines What You Are Willing To Endure. (#334)

358. Your Self-Portrait Determines Your Self-Conduct. (#11)

359. Your Significance Is Not In Your Similarity To Another, But In Your Point Of Difference From Another. (#54)

360. Your Success Is Decided By What You Are Willing To Ignore. (#17)

361. Your Tithe Is The Proof Of Your Trust. (#308)

362. Your Understanding Of God Determines Your Message To Men. (#302)

363. Your Unwillingness To Submit Deprives God Of The Authorization To Protect. (#355)

364. Your Unwillingness To Trust The Right Person Will Create More Losses Than Your Mistake Of Trusting The Wrong Person. (#64)

365. Your Words Are The Seeds For Feelings. (#61)

31 FACTS YOU SHOULD KNOW ABOUT WISDOM

1. Wisdom Is The Master Key To All The Treasures Of Life. (2 Chronicles 1:7-8, 10-12; Colossians 2:2-3)

2. Wisdom Is A Gift From God To You. (2 Samuel 2:3; Proverbs 2:6; Daniel 2:21; Ephesians 2:17; 1 Corinthians 12:8)

3. The Fear Of God Is The Beginning Of Wisdom. (Job 28:28; Psalm 111:10; Proverbs 9:10)

4. Jesus Is Made Unto Us Wisdom. (1 Corinthians 1:30; Ephesians 1:5, 8, 17)

5. The Holy Spirit Is The Spirit Of Wisdom That Unleashes Your Gifts. (Exodus 31:1, 3-4; Exodus 36:1; Daniel 1:4)

6. The Word Of God Is Able To Make You Wise Unto Salvation. (Psalm 107:43; John 5:39; 2 Timothy 3:15)

7. The Wisdom Of God Is Foolishness To The Natural Mind. (Proverbs 18:2; Isaiah 55:8-9; 1 Corinthians 2:4-5)

8. Your Conversation Reveals How Much Wisdom You Possess. (1 Kings 10:24; Proverbs 18:21; Proverbs 29:11; James 3:2)

9. The Wisdom Of This World Is A False Substitute For The Wisdom Of God. (1 Corinthians 2:4, 13; James 3:13-17)

10. All The Treasures Of Wisdom And Knowledge Are Hidden In Jesus Christ. (1 Corinthians 1:23-24; 1 Corinthians 2:7-8; Colossians 2:2-3)

11. The Word Of God Is Your Source Of Wisdom.
    (Deuteronomy 4:5-6; Psalm 119:98-100;
    Proverbs 2:6)
12. God Will Give You Wisdom When You Take The
    Time To Listen. (Proverbs 2:6; Isaiah 40:31;
    John 10:27; James 1:5)
13. Right Relationships Increase Your Wisdom.
    (Proverbs 13:20; 1 Corinthians 15:33;
    2 Thessalonians 3:6; 1 Timothy 6:5)
14. The Wisdom Of Man Is Foolishness To God.
    (1 Corinthians 1:20-21, 25; 1 Corinthians 3:19)
15. Men Of Wisdom Will Always Be Men Of Mercy.
    (Galatians 6:1; James 3:17; James 5:19-20)
16. Wisdom Is Better Than Jewels Or Money.
    (Job 28:18; Proverbs 3:13-15; Proverbs 8:11;
    Proverbs 16:16)
17. Wisdom Is More Powerful Than Weapons Of War.
    (Proverbs 12:6; Ecclesiastes 9:18; Isaiah 33:6;
    Acts 6:10)
18. The Mantle Of Wisdom Makes You 10 Times
    Stronger Than Those Without It. (Psalm 91:7;
    Ecclesiastes 7:19; Daniel 1:17, 20)
19. The Wise Hate Evil...The Evil Hate The Wise.
    (Proverbs 1:7, 22; Proverbs 8:13; Proverbs 9:8;
    Proverbs 18:2)
20. Wisdom Reveals The Treasure In Yourself.
    (Proverbs 19:8; Ephesians 2:10; Philippians 1:6;
    1 Peter 2:9-10)
21. The Proof Of Wisdom Is The Presence Of Joy And
    Peace. (Psalm 119:165; Proverbs 3:13;
    Ecclesiastes 7:12; James 3:17)
22. Wisdom Makes Your Enemies Helpless Against
    You. (Proverbs 16:7; Ecclesiastes 7:12;
    Isaiah 54:17; Luke 21:15)

23. Wisdom Creates Currents Of Favor And Recognition Toward You. (Proverbs 3:1, 4; Proverbs 4:8; Proverbs 8:34-35)

24. The Wise Welcome Correction. (Proverbs 3:11-12; Proverbs 9:8-9)

25. When The Wise Speak, Healing Flows. (Proverbs 10:11,20-21; Proverbs 12:18)

26. When You Increase Your Wisdom, You Will Increase Your Wealth. (Psalm 112:1,3; Proverbs 3:16; Proverbs 8:18, 21; Proverbs 14:24)

27. Wisdom Can Be Imparted By The Laying On Of Hands Of A Man Of God. (Deuteronomy 34:9; Acts 6:6, 8, 10; 2 Timothy 1:6, 14)

28. Wisdom Guarantees Promotion. (Proverbs 4:8-9; Proverbs 8:15-16; Ezra 7:25)

29. Wisdom Loves Those Who Love Her. (Proverbs 2:3-5; Proverbs 8:17, 21)

30. He That Wins Souls Is Wise. (Proverbs 11:30; Daniel 12:3; Romans 10:14-15)

31. Wisdom Will Be Given To You When You Pray For It In Faith. (Matthew 7:7-8, 11; James 1:5-6)

31 Days To Understanding Your Mentor, The Holy Spirit

━━━━━━━━━━━

1. The Holy Spirit Is A Person, Not A Dove, Wind Or Fire. (John 14:16)
2. The Holy Spirit Created You. (Job 33:4)
3. The Holy Spirit Is The Author Of All Scripture And The Inspiration Of All Scripture. (2 Timothy 3:16)
4. The Holy Spirit Confirms That Jesus Is Within You. (1 John 4:13)
5. The Holy Spirit Decides The Skills, Gifts And Talents Within You. (1 Corinthians 12:4-11)
6. The Holy Spirit Gives Life. (2 Corinthians 3:6)
7. The Holy Spirit Confirms You Are A Child Of God. (Romans 8:16)
8. The Holy Spirit Imparts A Personal Prayer Language That Dramatically Increases Your Strength And Faith. (Jude 1:20)
9. The Holy Spirit Talks To You. (Revelation 2:7)
10. The Holy Spirit Reveals The Truth You Need To Live Victoriously. (John 16:13)
11. The Holy Spirit Is The Source Of The Anointing... The Special Power Of God Given For Your Assignment. (Luke 4:18)
12. The Holy Spirit Is The Source Of Every Desired Emotion You Are Pursuing In Your Life. (Galatians 5:22-23)
13. The Holy Spirit Knows Every Detail Of The Purpose And Plan Of God For Your Life. (Romans 8:27-28)

14. The Holy Spirit Decides When You Are Ready To Be Tested. (Luke 4:1-2)
15. The Holy Spirit Is Your Intercessor On Earth. (Romans 8:26)
16. The Holy Spirit Loves Singing. (Psalm 100:1-2)
17. The Holy Spirit Is The Source Of Your Joy. (Psalm 16:11)
18. The Holy Spirit Is Your Only Source Of True Peace. (Galatians 5:22-23; Philippians 4:7)
19. The Holy Spirit Removes All Fear. (2 Timothy 1:7)
20. The Holy Spirit Shows You Pictures Of Your Future. (John 16:13; Acts 7:55)
21. The Holy Spirit Gives You The Necessary Love You Need Towards Others. (Romans 5:5)
22. The Holy Spirit Decides Your Assignment. (Acts 13:2-4)
23. The Holy Spirit Enables You To Enter Into The Kingdom Of God. (John 3:5-6)
24. The Holy Spirit Only Guides Those Who Are Sons Of God. (Romans 8:14)
25. The Holy Spirit Knows The Person To Whom You Have Been Assigned. (Acts 8:29)
26. The Holy Spirit Will Send Inner Warnings To Protect You From Wrong People And Places. (Acts 16:6-7)
27. The Holy Spirit Is Grieved And Saddened By Wrong Conduct. (Ephesians 4:30-31)
28. The Holy Spirit Critiques Every Moment, Motive And Movement Of Your Life. (Jeremiah 17:10)
29. The Holy Spirit Becomes An Enemy To The Rebellious. (Isaiah 63:10)
30. The Holy Spirit Withdraws When Offended. (Ephesians 4:30-32; Hosea 5:15)
31. The Holy Spirit Raised Jesus From The Dead, And He Will Raise You From The Dead When Christ Returns To The Earth. (Romans 8:11)

12 Ingredients Of The Perfect Day

"But the path of the just is as the shining light, that shineth more and more unto The Perfect Day."
(Proverbs 4:18)

1. **Preparation**...Of Your Mind, Spirit And Body.
2. **Meditation**...On The Law Of God, Our Wisdom.
3. **Motivation**...The Stirring Up Of Passion And Enthusiasm For Your Assignment.
4. **Organization**...Of Daily Schedule Of Appointments.
5. **Elimination**...Of Any Appointment Or Request That Does Not Qualify For Your Focus.
6. **Delegation**...Of Tasks To Others.
7. **Impartation**...From Your Mentors And To Protégés.
8. **Vocation**...The Problem You Are Assigned To Solve.
9. **Information**...The Pursuit Of Wisdom And Knowledge.
10. **Celebration**...Of Family And Those You Love.
11. **Documentation**...Journal Of Your Daily Experiences.
12. **Restoration**...Of Health Through Exercise And Sleep.

Your Daily Success Routine

1. Perfect Your Daily Success Routine. The Secret Of Your Future Is Hidden In Your Daily Routine.
2. Set A Specific Prayer Time In Your Secret Place To Meet With The Holy Spirit.
3. Listen Continually For The Voice Of Your Mentor, The Holy Spirit.
4. Write Your Daily Goals Down Every Day.
5. Document And Visualize Your Dreams And Goals.
6. Always Keep 25% Of Your Day Unscheduled To Allow For Unexpected Interruptions.

DECISION

DR. MIKE MURDOCK

1 Has embraced his Assignment to Pursue...Proclaim...and Publish the Wisdom of God to help people achieve their dreams and goals.

2 Preached his first public sermon at the age of 8.

3 Preached his first evangelistic crusade at the age of 15.

4 Began full-time evangelism at the age of 19, which has continued since 1966.

5 Has traveled and spoken to more than 16,000 audiences in 40 countries, including East and West Africa, the Orient, Europe and South America.

6 Noted author of over 200 books, including best sellers, *Wisdom for Winning, Dream Seeds, The Double Diamond Principle, The Law of Recognition* and *The Holy Spirit Handbook.*

7 Created the popular *Topical Bible* series for Businessmen, Mothers, Fathers, Teenagers; *The One-Minute Pocket Bible* series, and *The Uncommon Life* series.

8 The Creator of the Master 7 Mentorship Program, an Achievement Program for Believers.

9 Has composed thousands of songs such as "I Am Blessed," "You Can Make It," "God Rides On Wings Of Love" and "Jesus, Just The Mention Of Your Name," recorded by many gospel artists.

10 Is the Founder and Senior Pastor of The Wisdom Center, in Fort Worth, Texas...a Church with International Ministry around the world.

11 Host of *Wisdom Keys with Mike Murdock,* a weekly TV Program seen internationally.

12 Has appeared often on TBN, CBN, BET, Daystar, Inspirational Network, LeSea Broadcasting and other television network programs.

13 Has led over 3,000 to accept the call into full-time ministry.

THE MINISTRY

1 **Wisdom Books & Literature** - Over 200 best-selling Wisdom Books and 70 Teaching Tape Series.

2 **Church Crusades** - Multitudes are ministered to in crusades and seminars throughout America in "The Uncommon Wisdom Conferences." Known as a man who loves pastors, he has focused on church crusades for over 41 years.

3 **Music Ministry** - Millions have been blessed by the anointed songwriting and singing of Mike Murdock, who has made over 15 music albums and CDs available.

4 **Television** - *Wisdom Keys with Mike Murdock,* a nationally-syndicated weekly television program.

5 **The Wisdom Center** - The Church and Ministry Offices where Dr. Murdock speaks weekly on Wisdom for The Uncommon Life.

6 **Schools of The Holy Spirit** - Mike Murdock hosts Schools of The Holy Spirit in many churches to mentor believers on the Person and Companionship of The Holy Spirit.

7 **Schools of Wisdom** - In many major cities Mike Murdock hosts Schools of Wisdom for those who want personalized and advanced training for achieving "The Uncommon Dream."

8 **Missions Outreach** - Dr. Mike Murdock's overseas outreaches to 40 countries have included crusades in East and West Africa, the Orient, Europe and South America.

Millionaire-Talk

MIKE MURDOCK

31 THINGS You Will Need To Become A MILLIONAIRE

Your Financial Future Is Determined By The Instruction You Are Willing To Follow.

FREE BOOK ENCLOSED!

MASTER 7 MENTORSHIP PROGRAM *Mike Murdock*

DR. MIKE MURDOCK

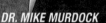

MY GIFT OF APPRECIATION
GIFT of Appreciation
Wisdom Is The Principal Thing

31 Things You Will Need To Become A Millionaire (2-CD's/WCPL-116)

Topics Include:

▷ You Will Need Financial Heroes
▷ Your Willingness To Negotiate Everything
▷ You Must Have The Ability To Transfer Your Enthusiasm, Your Vision To Others
▷ Know Your Competition
▷ Be Willing To Train Your Team Personally As To Your Expectations
▷ Hire Professionals To Do A Professional's Job

I have asked the Lord for 3,000 special partners who will sow an extra Seed of $58 towards our Television Outreach Ministry. Your Seed is so appreciated! Remember to request your Gift CD's, 2 Disc Volume, *31 Things You Will Need To Become A Millionaire,* when you write this week!

THE WISDOM CENTER 4051 Denton Highway • Fort Worth, TX 76117

1-817-759-BOOK
1-817-759-0300

You Will Love Our Website...!
www.WisdomOnline.com

A

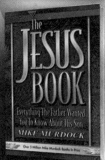

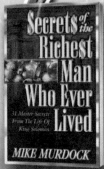

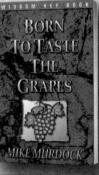

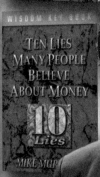

Career 7
Book Pak For Business People!

DR. MIKE MURDOCK

The Businessman's Topical Bible (Book/B-33/384pg/$10)

31 Secrets for Career Success (Book/B-44/114pg/$10)

31 Scriptures Every Businessman Should Memorize (Book/B-141/32pg/$3)

Seeds of Wisdom on Goal-Setting (Book/B-127/32pg/$5)

7 Rewards of Problem-Solving (Book/B-118/32pg/$7)

Seeds of Wisdom on Productivity (Book/B-137/32pg/$5)

The Mentor's Manna on Achievement (Book/B-79/32pg/$3)

ach Wisdom Book may be purchased separately if so desired.

THE WISDOM CENTER
4051 Denton Highway • Fort Worth, TX 76117

1-817-759-BOOK
1-817-759-0300

You Will Love Our Website...!
www.WisdomOnline.com

E

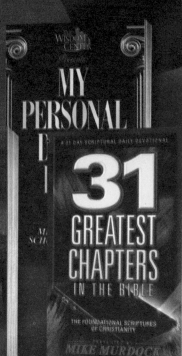

The CRISIS COLLECTION

You Get All 6 For One Great Price!

❶ **7 Keys For Surviving A Crisis** (DVD/MMPL-04D/$10)

❷ **You Can Make It!** (Music CD/MMML-05/$10)

❸ **Wisdom For Crisis Times** (6 Cassettes/TS-40/$30)

❹ **Seeds of Wisdom on Overcoming** (Book/B-17/32pg/$3)

❺ **Seeds of Wisdom on Motivating Yourself** (Book/B-171/32pg/$5)

❻ **Wisdom For Crisis Times** (Book/B-40/112pg/$9)

Also Included... Two Free Bonus Books!

*Each Wisdom Product may be purchased separately if so desired.

The Wisdom Center
The Crisis Collection
Only $**40**
Value
PAK-16
Wisdom Is The Principal Thing

Add 10% For S/H

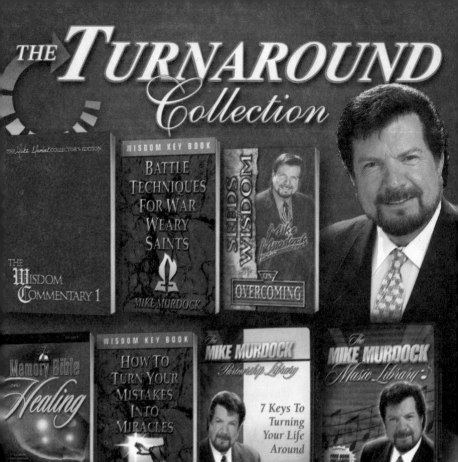

THE TURNAROUND Collection

- The Wisdom Commentary Vol. 1 (Book/B-136/256pg/52 Topics/$25)
- Battle Techniques For War-Weary Saints (Book/B-07/32pg/$5)
- Seeds of Wisdom on Overcoming (Book/B-17/32pg/$3)
- The Memory Bible on Healing (Book/B-196/32pg/$3)
- How To Turn Your Mistakes Into Miracles (Book/B-56/32pg/$5)
- 7 Keys To Turning Your Life Around (DVD/MMPL-03D/$10)
- The Sun Will Shine Again (Music CD/MMML-01/$10)

The Wisdom Center
The Turnaround Collection
Only $40 $61 Value
PAK-15
Wisdom Is The Principal Thing

Add 10% For S/H

ch Wisdom Product may be purchased separately if so desired.

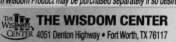

Favor 4!

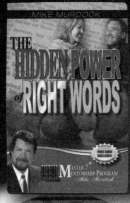

This Collection Of Wisdom Will Change The Seasons Of Your Life Forever!

1 The School of Wisdom #4 / 31 Keys To Unleashing Uncommon Favor...Tape Series (6 Cassettes/TS-44/$30)

2 The Hidden Power Of Right Words...
Master 7 Mentorship Program of Mike Murdock (CD/WCPL-27/$10)

3 7 Hidden Keys to Favor (Book/B-119/32pg/$7)

4 Seeds of Wisdom on Obedience (Book/B-20/32pg/$3)

The Wisdom Center
Favor 4 Collection!
Only $**35** $50 Value
PAK-12
Wisdom Is The Principal Thing

Add 10% For S/H

 THE WISDOM CENTER 4051 Denton Highway • Fort Worth, TX 76117

1-817-759-BOOK
1-817-759-0300

— You Will Love Our Website...! —
www.WisdomOnline.com

Financial $ecrets.

31 REASONS PEOPLE DO NOT RECEIVE THEIR FINANCIAL HARVEST
MIKE MURDOCK

The Wisdom Center
Buy One...
Receive The
Second One
FREE!
Wisdom Is The Principal Thing

VIDEO
7 KEYS to 1000 TIMES MORE
The Lord God Of Your Fathers
Make You A Thousand Times
So Many More As You Are,
And Bless You, As He Hath
Promised You!
Deuteronomy 1:11
MIKE MURDOCK

Your Financial World Will Change Forever.

Video 2-Pak!

8 Scriptural Reasons You Should Pursue Financial Prosperity

The Secret Prayer Key You Need When Making A Financial Request To God

The Weapon Of Expectation And The 5 Miracles It Unlocks

How To Discern Those Who Qualify To Receive Your Financial Assistance

How To Predict The Miracle Moment God Will Schedule Your Financial Breakthrough

Habits Of Uncommon Achievers

The Greatest Success Law I Ever Discovered

How To Discern Your Place Of Assignment, The Only Place Financial Provision Is Guaranteed

3 Secret Keys In Solving Problems For Others

The Wisdom Center
Video 2-Pak!
Only $30 $60 Value
VIPAK-01
Wisdom Is The Principal Thing

Add 10% For S/H

THE WISDOM CENTER
4051 Denton Highway • Fort Worth, TX 76117

1-817-759-BOOK
1-817-759-0300

—You Will Love Our Website...!—
www.WisdomOnline.com

K

THE WISDOM BIBLE

Partnership Edition

Over 120 Wisdom Study Guides Included Such As:

- ▶ 10 Qualities Of Uncommon Achievers
- ▶ 18 Facts You Should Know About The Anointing
- ▶ 21 Facts To Help You Identify Those Assigned To You
- ▶ 31 Facts You Should Know About Your Assignment
- ▶ 8 Keys That Unlock Victory In Every Attack
- ▶ 22 Defense Techniques To Remember During Seasons Of Personal Attack
- ▶ 20 Wisdom Keys And Techniques To Remember During An Uncommon Battle
- ▶ 11 Benefits You Can Expect From God
- ▶ 31 Facts You Should Know About Favor
- ▶ The Covenant Of 58 Blessings
- ▶ 7 Keys To Receiving Your Miracle
- ▶ 16 Facts You Should Remember About Contentious People
- ▶ 5 Facts Solomon Taught About Contracts
- ▶ 7 Facts You Should Know About Conflict
- ▶ 6 Steps That Can Unlock Your Self-Confidence
- ▶ And Much More!

Your Partnership makes such a difference in The Wisdom Center Outreach Ministries. I wanted to place a Gift in your hand that could last a lifetime for you and your family...**The Wisdom Study Bible.**

40 Years of Personal Notes...this Partnership Edition Bible contains 160 pages of my Personal Study Notes...that could forever change your Bible Study of The Word of God. This **Partnership Edition...**is my personal **Gift of Appreciation** when you sow your Sponsorship Seed of $1,000 to help us complete The Prayer Center and TV Studio Complex. An Uncommon Seed Always Creates An Uncommon Harvest!

Mike

Thank you from my heart for your Seed of Obedience (Luke 6:38).

This Gift Of
Appreciation Will Change
Your Bible Study For
The Rest Of Your Life.

The Wisdom Bible

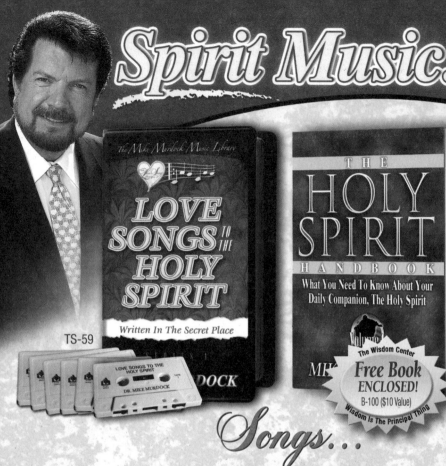

Spirit Music...

The Mike Murdock Music Library

LOVE SONGS TO THE HOLY SPIRIT
Written In The Secret Place

TS-59

THE HOLY SPIRIT HANDBOOK
What You Need To Know About Your Daily Companion, The Holy Spirit

MURDOCK

DR. MIKE MURDOCK

The Wisdom Center
Free Book ENCLOSED!
B-100 ($10 Value)
Wisdom Is The Principal Thing

Songs...

1. A Holy Place
2. Anything You Want
3. Everything Comes From You
4. Fill This Place With Your Presence
5. First Thing Every Morning
6. Holy Spirit, I Want To Hear You
7. Holy Spirit, Move Again
8. Holy Spirit, You Are Enough
9. I Don't Know What I Would Do Without You
10. I Let Go (Of Anything That Stops Me)
11. I'll Just Fall On You
12. I Love You, Holy Spirit
13. I'm Building My Life Around You
14. I'm Giving Myself To You
15. I'm In Love! I'm In Love!
16. I Need Water (Holy Spirit, You're My Well)
17. In The Secret Place
18. In Your Presence, I'm Always Changed
19. In Your Presence (Miracles Are Born)
20. I've Got To Live In Your Presence
21. I Want To Hear Your Voice
22. I Will Do Things Your Way
23. Just One Day At A Time
24. Meet Me In The Secret Place
25. More Than Ever Before
26. Nobody Else Does What You Do
27. No No Walls!
28. Nothing Else Matters Anymore (Since I've Been In The Presence Of You Lord)
29. Nowhere Else
30. Once Again You've Answered
31. Only A Fool Would Try (To Live Without You)
32. Take Me Now
33. Teach Me How To Please You
34. There's No Place I'd Rathe
35. Thy Word Is All That Matter
36. When I Get In Your Presenc
37. You're The Best Thing (Tha Ever Happened To Me)
38. You Are Wonderful
39. You've Done It Once
40. You Keep Changing Me
41. You Satisfy

The Wisdom Center
6 Tapes / Only $30*
PAK007
Wisdom Is The Principal Thing

Add 10% For S/H

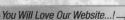

 THE WISDOM CENTER
4051 Denton Highway • Fort Worth, TX 76117

1-817-759-BOOK
1-817-759-0300

You Will Love Our Website...!
www.WisdomOnline.com

YOUR ASSIGNMENT IS YOUR DISTINCTION FROM OTHERS.

Assignment 4 Book Pak!

Uncommon Wisdom For Discovering Your Life Assignment.

❶ The Dream & The Destiny
Vol 1 (Book/B-74/164 pg/$12)

❷ The Anointing & The Adversity
Vol 2 (Book/B-75/192 pg/$12)

❸ The Trials & The Triumphs
Vol 3 (Book/B-97/160 pg/$12)

❹ The Pain & The Passion
Vol 4 (Book/B-98/144 pg/$12)

Each Wisdom Book may be purchased separately if so desired.

The Wisdom Center
Assignment 4 Book Pak!
Only $**30** $45 Value
WBL-14
Wisdom Is The Principal Thing

Add 10% For S/H

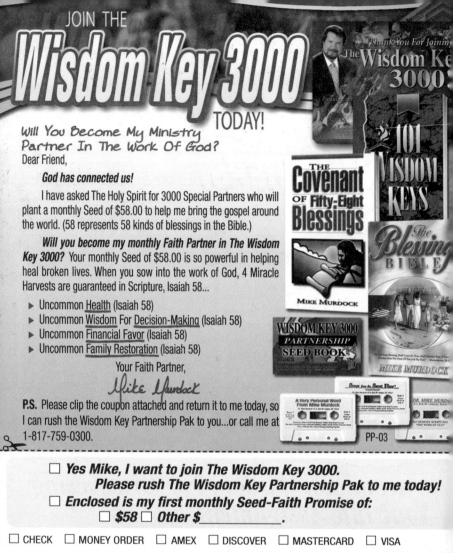